For
Martin Joseph and Russell Eugene
...who they were, who I am

And
Daniel Krozen
...an insufficient alternative if there isn't another Danny

Patina Soul

poems by Darrin James

First Printing, 2020

ISBN: 978-1-7349523-0-8

Cover photo by Nikki Roman

Cover design by Miles Darrin McMahon.

PROVIDENCE HILL
PUBLISHING

Acknowledgments

Thanks to:

Nikki Roman for the cover photo...that was a helluva weekend... right? Thanks for sharing in the ride.

My brother of brothers, Miles Darrin McMahon, cover designer extraordinaire, love yah forever. I've got your back any day, anywhere, any time.

Erica Lynn is that incredible person that anyone should consider themselves fortunate to know. I am fortunate to consider her a friend. Thank you for always putting up with me and pushing my dreams. You and I both know how hard you worked on and pushed for this collection. I will forever be grateful.

Robert Louis Henry at Right Hand Publishing was the missing piece that brought this to the finish line. Your expertise and effort is greatly appreciated.

Contents

Foreword – Patina Soul 1

Racing Thing 3

The Home 7

Cents of the Colliery 9

At The Wheel 11

Beer We Never Drank 14

Gypsy 16

Blueberry Beer 18

Bullwark 25

Aspire 27

Hollers 30

Who Turned Out The Town 34

American Tragedy 38

Bones 40

Lilacs 41

Nashville 43

Camaro 46

Monster Truck 49

Cast Lots 53

The Night We Met 57

Pennies 59

Dogs and Angels 61

218B 64

Public Radio 67

Remedy 69

Danny 71

Out There 72

Little Red Dog 74

Battlefield Youth 76

Rockingham 79

Walnut 83

Boxes 85

Green Flash 89

Foreword – Patina Soul

It seems that I wasn't given a new soul when souls were being assigned.

I don't do "new" very well.

I'm a sucker for the old – always have been. I wax poetic for the nostalgic. I relish the well-worn and competition proven over trend of the minute new technology. I like dirty. To a fault I like wrinkled. I'd rather have a "needs some work" tattered piece with a tale than factory-fresh with its warranties, guarantees; grandpa's cabin over your tract house; a frosty-faced, three-legged dog over a designer pup; a faded Sandy's Bar t-shirt over the polo everyone else is wearing.

In reflection, I come to the realization that this is the way I've always been.

As a child I remember going to those Sunday afternoon American Legion car shows. In those transition years between pedal cars and a Cinderella drivers' license it was never the gaudy hot rods with too much misplaced billet that impressed me, proved memorable. Instead, the un-restored, un-molested, unique, used everyday cars were what drew my attention. Retired men have all the time to preen and polish their identical chrome bumpers and count the layers of clear coat over fresh metal flake, but it's only time, experiences, weather that brings about unique patina. There's a story behind a dent in the fender, peeling Dolly Parton bumper sticker, scratch in the paint – the overall patina.

Patina, I would maintain, is the color of age, the hue resulting from time wearing down what was once new, pristine, and shiny. As such, the following collection represents the subtle events in life that stains a soul, weathers a soul, for one reason or another that has caused a patina to cover a soul. Patina is not moldy rot. It is not cancerous rust. It is not a cataclysmic event that violently batters and grotesquely distorts. It the gentle wearing down, the staining, the slow erosion – call it life, call it "coming of age," call it jaded – I choose to describe them as the patina on my soul.

There's a certain beauty in patina. As it hides nothing, it shows what it truly is, even if some consider what they see as faults, flaws.

There's a freedom in patina. The new has worn off. Where something new and pristine may be kept unused in a safe place, so to maintain its newness, the intent of something new is to be used and not kept new forever.

There's a story in patina and that's what's led us here.

Racing Thing

"You aren't going to do that racing thing… are you?"
Was that a question?
Phrased as such,
but maybe not so much.
Closer to a statement,
a guised command.
As if any boy could ever understand
the nuancing of an old man.

Pause.
As the old man looked off.

                                Distant.

Boys don't understand
when they are supposed to give a certain answer.
Boys are brash.
Boys own the world.
It is not wealth,
nor power,
prestige,
nor knowledge
that carries the day.
It is ambivalent youth
which rules the world
At least in the minds
of those who believe
that they rule the world.

With that mind,
not thinking of consequence,
nor meaning,
nor intent,
of the old man's words,
the boy answered:

"If the opportunity came up, I would."

Boys say these things
because boys only see trophies.
Boys can't see past oversized checks and
    blondes who present them.
Boys don't see the Armco.
Boys don't fully understand what rapid deceleration
    does to a body, inside a body.

Boys only see victory lane,
    where the champagne rains.
Boys don't see emergency rooms
    where the blood spills.
Boys don't see funeral parlors
    where tears fall.
                        But old men do.

Because old men have.

It is because of this sage wisdom,
that old men try to enlighten boys
and enlightened they would be
if boys were smart enough to listen.

Once a brash boy himself,
the old man realized he needed to be more blunt
for the sake of this boy who now owns the world he once did.
So he says, still looking into the distance:

"Don't do it; you'll get yourself killed,"

And nothing more.

In his mind,
in the silence,
the boy laughed
as boys have done,
as long as there have been boys,
dreaming of immortality
through racing fame.

In his mind,
in the silence
the old man, wistful
with his long look at the distance
saw his kid brother
whom he had been raising as his own
until he was lost
in a high-speed car
crash
on the road to the lake
when he was just sitting still.

Unspeakable.
As if advice from old men to boys
is ever heard.

Short years later,
opportunity arose.
The boy found himself in a Pontiac
and a Chevrolet found his door.
A helmet found the post
and the boy took the trophy
but forgot the check at the track
realized only in the morning light
when the boy found himself older,
aching,
unable to silence his ears,
unable to focus,
unable to speak clearly,
as if anyone was listening anyway.

The Home

The Home.
That's what it was called.
Not "Nursing Home,"
not "Care Home,"
not "Old Folks' Home,"
just "The Home."
Despite this moniker,
there was nothing "home" about it,
yet I spent every day there
with my younger brothers
the summer I turned nine
watching my grandfather wither
away
unable to speak,
unable to feed himself.
We watched our mother care for him,
feed him.
Unable to move his head,
she hacked a notch in a plastic cup
so it would fit around his nose,
when she raised it to his lips.

Those who consider that dying with dignity
can shove it straight up their ass.

The lingering question remains:
"Where did they hide the devil?"
as that place was hell
evident enough

DARRIN JAMES

to children,
to four-, six-, and eight-year-old boys,
the summer they turned five, seven, and nine,
just old enough to barely comprehend,
just old enough for the experience to be formative,
skewing or setting straight a kid's view on life.

Only years later were we able to talk about it,
talk about The Home.
I do not have a living will,
but I've made this much known
to the brothers I spent that summer with:
Do not let me end up there.
By whatever means necessary
do not let me get to The Home.
No matter the sin you must commit
as paying a penance in purgatory
would be a more painless course
than that of another summer in The Home.

Cents of the Colliery

the stub stamped "Colliery"
fell from the heirloom box.
John—mom's maiden name.
September '35.
forty hours of black lung labor
at fifty-nine and three-quarter cents an hour
makes twenty-three ninety for the week.
"but that was good money back then."
something about a great depression
         I could never figure out
         what was so great about depression.

"Mom, who is this?"
lineage unclear a short century later.
"He was the one,"
she says,
"they found down here along the road."

ah.
yes.
He, the whispered family story.

He the one, They found
with a "hole" in the back of his head.
what remained of that twenty-dollar check
less the groceries he was carrying
missing
         gone

DARRIN JAMES

she wouldn't say *killed*.
not in this town.
not in that supposed better time.
not down at the end of the road,
the only road
this family has called "the road" for generations.
killed
for a sack of groceries
and what remained of a cent-splitting paycheck
"that was good money back then"
sure.
okay
but bread is bread and a life is a life.
nevermind the century.
        nevermind the currency.
                man-made concepts of counting and control.
but a life…

nothing was solved
        no punishment levied
                and the story,
                        His whispered story
is forgotten,
                                grows silent

        as time passes
and coal to ashes,
ashes to dust,
and the cosmic winds
rush in
then on
to infinity.

At The Wheel

these mountains were supposed to be easy.
after Da Nang,
twenty-five years
after Da Nang,
anything else should have been easy.

then a mid-September morning,
                Saturday morning,
you gotta pull him away from those CBS cartoons,
explain to a seven-year-old that
they don't walk away like the movies,
     at a place on 87 not too far west of here.
explain to him what happened in the
overnight to his best friend's dad,
     just coming home from work.
Explain to him *asleep at the wheel,*
     in a dell between these mountains
     that were supposed to be easy.

he cries—
     expected in this unexpected.
let him.
when he stops to catch his breath:
"let's go for a ride."

             were we just confirming the news?
let a boy figure it out for himself.
             validating the unfathomable?
let a boy figure out that the world isn't easy.

           when the world was supposed to be innocent.
let a boy figure out that life isn't fair.
            was that the life lesson we were looking for?

park that grey Oldsmobile alongside 87
with a view down the drive
between the pine trees and the garage
where the red and white tow trucks
drag the wrecks.

let that boy look into that tow yard
and let him confirm with his own eyes
that the smashed to hell Ford he's looking at
is his best friend's dad's work truck,
a truck the boy rode in weeks before
down that very road
over that very spot.
and the boy looks,
and the boy studies,
and the boy says,
      because he's still a boy,
      and he's hopeful,
      and innocent,
      and seven,
      and twenty minutes ago didn't have a care in the world
      other than Ninja Turtles cartoons,
"that doesn't look so bad, right Dad?"
      because the boy doesn't know about the world.
the boy's thinking the world has it wrong.
"right Dad?"

come Monday morning, you wake before dawn
microwave the water for your instant coffee,
check on your still sleeping sons,
shackle into your steel toes
then fire that Olds
for that long, quiet drive
through those mountains
out 87, east of town,
thinking of old mountains.
no mountains are easy,
no mountains are smooth,
knowing these mountains are tough
as all mountains are.

DARRIN JAMES

Beer We Never Drank

We never drank that beer, did we?

Thinking about it now,
I can't seem to remember.
        Was it beer we even bought?

Whatever it was, we didn't drink that night… right?

We dropped your cousin off and then you, me,
And we didn't kiss
        that regrettable void remains irrefutable,
And I went north
        in the red car.
And you went south
        in yours.
And I'd see you once after that
        before I left for good.
And once again
        before you took his name.

Playing this timeline in black on white, a new found clarity, an
unwavering certainty that we didn't drink whatever the alcohol
was that had seemed so important that we took a random exit in
Jersey and drove around trying to find anyone who would sell the
stuff.

Marie—that lightning coming across 80
as we bootlegged over the Gap.
Remember that lightning?
Helluva day that was.
And we never even got into that beer.

I will open one tonight, with that bar-stolen bottle opener,
toast the heavens for no good reason other
        than they seem closer than you've been,
then pitch the cap off the balcony.

I wonder the dent a bottle cap makes from fifteen stories up.
Does it make a dent at all?
Or does it just blow away?

Blown away.

    Wishes never granted.
        Dreams never told.
            Memories with no recall.
            Beer we never drank.

Gypsy

And I looks at the gypsy and I says,
I says,
I says, "I love you."
And the gypsy looks at me and says,
The gypsy looks at me and says,
she looks at me and she says,
she says, "I never loved you…

.....I could never love you."

That.

That is what the gypsy says.

Spin.
Spin faster.
Like a cork pulled out of the tub on a Saturday night.

Spin.
And the gurgle as all that the stopper held in is let out and it can't
keep up with itself on the way to the sewer to pool with all the piss
and the shit, never to be anything more than appalling ever again.

Spin.

And the gypsy leaves the car
and cooly, calmly, coldly shuts the door
without another word,
leaves me idling outside her parents' summer house,
leaves me and the Plymouth idling there in the drive
without a word.

Spin.
As the small block internals revolve a thousand times a minute.

Spin.
A thousand years from now,
they will identify not only the death of a body
but also the death of what we now call "soul."
When the future invents that word,
apply it to this instance of mine.

Spin.
Glad now she shut the door so methodically,
so tightly.
As the car begins to fill with the emotion
from the holes she riddled in me
and I begin to drown in them.

Spin.
she could have made it painless.
she could have just heaved a grenade.
But this one.
Ah this one.
This.
she wanted it to hurt.
she wanted to feel the dagger split the skin.
she wanted to feel the splash of the spurt.
she wanted not to kill me,
she wanted only to make me bleed 'til my kingdom come.
A wound to make me relive her every day.
One that makes me distrust the world
for what I felt for the gypsy.

Blueberry Beer

Six packa blueberry beer.
Glass bottles on the beach.
Breaking all the rules, down the shore.
Ah, but everything was alright.
     Jersey shore, late July.

Late night, at the edge of the dunes,
staring out at the black Atlantic
with the fishing boat lights bobbing out there.
Only a ghost from a Springsteen song coulda found us
buried in the sand, drinking that blueberry beer.
     Her choice, her acquisition.
     I wouldn't have picked it.
        She thought it was worth a try.

Ah… yeah… it was worth a try.

Then a troop train got me
     Took me far, far away.
Hers,
     the letters I remember most.
Hers,
     the concern most sincere.
Hers,
     the conversation I found solace in.
And then…

Then a troop transport got me
     took me even farther away.

And then…

The poet's story?
        We drifted
                like fishing boats
                        night trolling off Jersey.

The true story?
        I cut the lines.
        I severed the moorings.
        I pushed off.
        Pushed off hard.
        Threw wake in the no wake zone.
        Didn't look back.

And a pause here
        because I didn't expect to get here,
didn't know this was a place,
        didn't know this memory so vivid,
                didn't know this emotion was here.

I didn't…

I've broken hearts,
        never maliciously,
but I've broken hearts.
        I… I'm not proud of it.

In my mind that girl and I,
        we were never officially anything
other than damn good friends
        But…

DARRIN JAMES

Alone tonight,
        staring out at the dark Pacific,
I am overwhelmed,
        I am overcome.

Her heart
        out of all the hearts
is the one I wish I hadn't broken.

I am a dumb boy
        as boys have been known to be
when it comes to matters of the heart.
        This I realize tonight.

If this finds you,
        and you know exactly who you are —
God, I'm not even sure I want it to —
        But if it does, if this does find you,
wherever you have drifted to,
whatever life has snagged in your lines,
        please consider this an apology
        from a dumb boy
        who, because he is a dumb boy, cannot just say,
        "I'm sorry."
        from a dumb boy
        who only now has begun to realize what he has done.

        You were right.
        Like blueberry beer, we were worth a try.

It is my heart that breaks tonight.

Since that night,
	that July, Jersey beach night,
fate has plied me with blueberry beer
	twice
and it gave me heartburn
	each time.

C's –
There's a bootleg
of That song
from That show
That night.

You can see us on the tape –
my red ball cap rising above the assembled
you pressed against me
together
leading the congregation
leading a ballpark full of the faithful in
their song,
their story,
their anthem…
it's their prayer.

But you
and I
both damn well know
it's not their song,
that's our song.

That's a lie.

It's your song.

Always has been
since that night –
the blueberry beer night.

C's, it always will be.

I cannot hear that track
without being in that five minutes and fifty-one seconds with you.

I can't hear
the roar
when those opening notes hit
the raw emotional cries of the Jersey girls
without feeling you pressed against me,
feeling how you swayed,
how you just took it in.

In that moment
I was closer to you
than I have ever been
to anyone
at any single moment
in this life of mine.

C's
I knew what you were thinking,
knew what you were feeling,
knew what you wanted me to do,
which is what I should have done.

PATINA SOUL

I should have kissed you.

Dammit.

I should have kissed you.

I should have kissed you
and I didn't kiss you
and that's my regret.

I should have kissed you
and I didn't kiss you.
That's why a man hates
the boy that he was.

Should have kissed you,
didn't kiss you,
and it's taken these years,
these long, lonely years
to realize how
badly
I botched the whole fucking thing.

And now?

Man...

C's –

I don't expect you to understand
I...
just...

DARRIN JAMES

I just want you to know
that I think of you
as I wander these miles in between
I dwell on life that could have been
where on a Saturday night
we'd be
singing…

'

Bullwark

Your dad was in the war?
Yeah, mine was in it too.
Naw, he don't talk about it.
Says he wishes he never knew…

Anchors aweigh!
Give 'er the gun.
Freedom ain't free,
Fortunate Son.

Bunker buster.
Bombs away!
You or them.
Hell to pay.

Bullwark.
Beachhead.
Bastion.
Shoot 'em dead.

Take that hill.
Take that ridge.
Take that field.
Burn that bridge.

Under fire.
Overseas.
Find your God.
No more ease.

DARRIN JAMES

Cannon ball.
Roadside bomb.
Normandy.
Vietnam.

Burning in deserts.
Buried in a bog.
Demons and angels
Get lost in the fog.

Rockets are red.
Tracers, gleaming.
Pull the trigger.
Silence screaming.

Fill the bags.
Dog tag toes.
Name. Number.
So it goes.

Flags on boxes.
Twenty-one guns.
Riderless horse.
Fatherless sons.

Yeah, my dad was in the war.
Yours was over there too.
They don't talk about it.
I wish they never knew.

Aspire

Four forty-five in the morning
a message lights the screen.

He does this to me once—twice—a year.
Odd hours questions,
odd hours thoughts.
He's thinking,
thinking about moving,
thinking about getting out.
Again.

What sparked it this time?
What job let him go?
What payment went unpaid?
Who turned him down at it the bar?
Maybe the bar wasn't even open.
Hasn't been open.
No sense in burning the lights
With no one around.

Young men don't aspire anymore.
They want.
They lust.
They accept.
They settle.
They RSVP to life, with regrets,
but they don't aspire,
not like they once did,
not like he still does.

DARRIN JAMES

I get his messages
at the most predictably unpredictable times.
I get his messages
because I am the one who got farthest away
and he wants to know what it's like out there,
     out here.

He always wanted to get out.
The Corps was going to pave his path.
The Corps was the only road he saw out
and guidance counselors don't try
to change
redneck kid's minds.
They don't offer other options,
don't show maps to other paths,
just pats on the back –
better him in the sandbox
than a kid with a chance.

At the recruiters strip mall office
they givvum the t-shirt,
     and a ship-out date,
     and a town, it gives its farewells,
        and a girl gives herself for a night,
          and a nation gives token thanks.

And the Corps gives him a beating,
     and the boy gives it his all
     until that boy breaks,
     until his body breaks.

And the Corps said he couldn't be fixed.
So they sign his papers and send him home.
>No benefits.
>No prospects.
>No way out.
>So it goes.

And a community that once sang his praises
>whispers their "what went wrongs".
And that girl?
>Mother to somebody's other.
And the nation he'da given his life for
>forgets he raised his hand.

Years pass
at an ever-accelerating rate,
and once every now and again
he asks
he asks about
>out there,
>out here.
He yearns for
>out there,
>out here.

>I used to think we were all going to be President,
>>have everything we ever wanted to have.
>>>Now I see so few
>>can even make payment on the dream.

>>The generation that screamed "YOLO"
>>>struggles to see
>>how little living they are doing,
>>how little living they will ever do.

DARRIN JAMES

Hollers

The cosmos collided in that moment
sending fate and providence,
chance, maybe luck,
riding angels wings down my way,
pulling me away from my post,
putting that phone in my grasp,
seeing it glow with his name
the instant it touched my hand.

He didn't have to say what he was talking about.
I knew from his tone was he was fixin' to do,
        what he was thinking about… again.
But how do you ease into that
        when you don't have time to ease?

"Just slow down,"
        not just his talking.
                Ranting,
                        broken explanations.
        Not just the voices in his mind,
                their ranting,
                        their broken explanations
                                telling him to do, what he keeps
                                        saying he's going to do
                                                without saying it.
        I need him to slow down that truck,
            not just for his safety,
                not for the safety of an oncoming unfortunate.
        I need him to slow that truck down

because I knew
       I only had so long.
       So long before "so long."
       So long before he drove into one a them hollers
       where the signal,
       this life line,
       would drop.
"Bud, just stop the truck; let's talk."
       Because I knew
       once that last bar dropped
       he wouldn't be able to hear me
       and I couldn't him.
       I'd be a helpless million miles away
       and he'd be alone with his demons.
       My best friend,
       alone with his demons,
       back in them dark hollers.

He's got his reasons.
       He's rattling them off
       and I'm telling him it'll work out.
       Just give me the time to get there.
       I'll be back home this time next week.
       We'll figure it out then.
       "We'll figure this out, bud, just tell me where…"
And he's sayin' "no"
       as the line crackles
       as the dark road
       carries him back inta them hollers.

DARRIN JAMES

The callback goes to voicemail.
      Was that it? The last?
Call back.
      As it rings:
      The realization of how long it's
      been since that place was home
      presented now in the notion
      that I don't know anyone to call on his behalf.
To voicemail.
Call back.
First ring.
      Second…
His voice answers,
faint, unfocused,
but still his voice.
      "Where yah at bud?"
      Based on a common history,
      I have an inkling the road he's on.
            There's only a few where the signal comes back…
      "No. Not this time. I'm not doing that this time…
            I'm doing it this time."
      As the call drops again
      as the road leads him deeper into them hollers.

The redial to voicemail.
         The second… voicemail.
                Three.
      Now four.
      Now despair.

Can't call 911.
    Not from a million miles away.
Can't call a dispatcher who doesn't know the hollers.

Call the main desk at the police station.
    Area code, exchange we grew up in.
Trooper So-and-So.
    Here's the deal… got this call,
    million miles away.
    I understand needles and haystacks,
    chasing ghosts,
    catching smoke,
    but I got no other option.
No… I don't think he's got a gun.
That doesn't sound like him.
No… I don't know where he's staying.
Somewhere off the mountain, maybe by the bridge.
No… I don't know for sure what he's driving.
But I'd put money he's in his little red Dodge.
No… I don't know where he's going, would go, could go.
He might be on that inkling road,
But I'm not sure.
I just know he's down off the mountains.
I just know he's in them hollers now.

And the trooper says he'll go for a ride.
    A hopeful statement with a tone of despair.
See if he can see anything.
    As if anything can be seen, up in them dark hollers.
Says he'll call me… either way…
    And here I am,
        still waiting on that call.

DARRIN JAMES

Who Turned Out The Town

This was once a magical place of wonder,
where boyhood dreams came true.
We fought, we raced, we dreamed;
we learned, we played, we grew.

Never did I think I'd leave,
have a need to plan my time "back,"
but a troop train took me out of here,
and that's one helluva long track.

But "back" is where I find myself,
homestead front porch with that view,
Trying to adjust to time zone changes
in the quiet with a cold Pottsville brew.

And I look out over the mountains,
from there I should be able to see kingdom come.
But all I see is darkness—
coal, tar, soot, shadows, spades, raven, glum.

Man, I know it's been a minute,
but I distinctly remember a glow
that would rise above those mountains,
a light for the world to know,
that there was a little town down there
where lives were takin' place
but, there now seems to be none of that,
just a void out there in space.

From the light on Saint Basil's steeple
to the 60-watt in the West Main phone booth,
to that Texaco star hangin' at the mini-mart
over the drag race stop light of my youth,
there had always been a glow from there,
a guiding light to be found,
so silently I wonder to myself,
"Who the hell turned out the town?"

And I run through a list of pranksters,
those capable of shutting off the lights.
It was never their intent to be malicious,
you know—kids get bored at night.
But they've all grown-up, been locked up
or moved on down the road,
chasing paychecks somewhere else
in a different area code.

I'd go over and see a buddy,
one who I used to race,
but there isn't opportunity 'round here,
so he moved on to another place.
I'd ask the smartest girl I'd ever known,
but she put on a gown,
and her husband moved her to those city lights
right outta this dark, old town.

At the bar, I'd buy a round for he who could tell
why the town is dark at night,
but the local couldn't pay their bills,
neon's dark, doors locked up tight.
There ain't a human out there,

neither a friend nor stranger to be found.
But still I yell, "Can anybody hear me?
Hey! Who turned out the town?"

Now, I rise from my chair, lager in my hand,
thinking it must have been my seat.
Maybe if I stand, get some elevation,
I'll see it from my feet.
But, man, I ain't seein' nuthin'
except the stars up in the sky,
the moon, and a big, old jet airliner
with no reason to stop, flyin' by.

I want to wake up my mother, and in a panic, ask her,
"When'd it get so dark?"
What the hell happened to my hometown;
how the hell did it lose its spark?
I didn't see any power lines dropped
or poles layin' on the ground,
Ain't no transformers burnin' tonight,
so who turned out the town?

You know, maybe it's my memory,
maybe my memory got it wrong.
Maybe this town was always this dark,
maybe the lights were never on.
Maybe it was youthful wonder,
hope, that always made it glow.
Maybe it's not darkness that is the enemy,
maybe it's time who is my foe.

My mother wants me to stay this time,
doesn't want me goin' back,
wants to see me weld myself
to that smalltown circle track.
But Momma, there ain't no jobs 'round here,
ain't worth putting roots down.
Even if I stayed to fight,
nobody wants to turn back on the town.

I had a dream the other night when everything was still.
I swore I saw my hometown risin' 'bove them hills.
Business was a boomin', storefronts all glowed bright,
then I realized I was just dreamin'; it was just the morning light.

DARRIN JAMES

American Tragedy

I cried aloud when I saw the name.
Headlines all about him,
small town judgement levied,
on a grey, autumn Sunday afternoon.

We were boys together
up on those cold quiet mountains.
Shared a classroom, shared a lunchroom table,
an alma mater—sweet be thy memory.

I defend him to this day as being one of the good ones.
That's how I remember that kid,
oft wondering what happened,
never having kept in touch, so life goes.

Which leads me here,
staring at his name in the report,
not believing it to be true,
doubting the headlines, asking:

"What leads a man to rob the dollar store
at gunpoint
on a Sunday morning
before the churches even open their doors?"

His wife, his child's mother,
at the wheel of the getaway car.
They didn't get far, they never do,
not from my hometown.

I can picture the scene
yet struggle to understand
that level of desperation
on a Sunday morning.

It was the dollar store, for God's sake.
On a Sunday morning, for heaven's sakes.
The law is the law, but I cannot condemn,
could not convict that level of desperation.

He couldn't have been looking to get rich,
not at an Appalachian dollar store on a Sunday morn'.
I can only imagine there was a bill to be paid,
a pain to be pilled away,
a mouth to be fed, just trying to break even, not even get ahead.

When it gets that bad,
aren't we all to blame?
When a man has to resort to this,
don't we all lose?

Heart breaks, mind spins.
Minimum sentence... not for this kid.
He was one of the good ones; I just don't understand.
He was one of the good ones; I still believe this to be true.

Abject desperation
for the American Dream
proves once again
to be the truest American tragedy.

Bones

those were our parents' bones we dug up that night.
weren't they?
dug up
and laughed at
then tossed to the fire we drank around,
saying:
"what good is tonight
for anything other than this?
we'll get to living in the morning."

then we woke,
sore and still stoned
cold
as the fire had gone out
as fires always do.
only then did we realize
the ash from the bones we burned
was breathed in.
now part of us,
the cruel fate that befell the predecessors
would be ours
sooner than we could know.

Lilacs

She smelled of lilacs.

For the last twenty minutes, the scent wasn't present, at least wasn't noted, but now lying in the still of the night with the glow of the city shining through the window, illuminating the room, the distinct fragrance graced my olfactory, and I was a child again.

In that instant, I was back in my grandfather's yard, in that springtime sun, waiting for whatever innocent children wait for on the northern facing slopes of Endless Mountains. There, I was running around that lilac bush where his driveway intersected the road, planting my nose on and taking deep whiffs of those purple flowers, the source of that smell that filled the mountain air.

Lying alongside her sweat-soaked body, arm resting on her chest, feeling it rising and falling softly in that calm, the world rushing back together, the pieces momentarily forgotten returning to form a complete picture, and me, staring at the ceiling, at the shadows the popcorn they plaster up there to hide the imperfections make. Is she contently asleep, peacefully off to the dreamland I'd hope to give her someday? Or is she just lying there, staring off at the ceiling on our lives? I don't bother enough to look, content to feign sleep rather than spark conversation in the still.

When I was a child, my father would come in and check on me in the morning before he'd leave for work. His footsteps on the carpet, the soft rattle of the handle as he opened the door, the pause as I assume he looked in—as I never bothered to look, content to feign sleep rather than answer questions—the click of the latch and a hollow rattle as the door closed, retreating footsteps, the thud of the sliding door, the Oldsmobile comes to life, then decrescendo as he drove away back to quiet, back to dreams.

DARRIN JAMES

In the morning, I will take two shots from the medicine bottle, spit in the sink what I cannot force down my throat and stare at the man who stares back at me, although his stare becomes more sullen, more slack as the calendar slips the days as opportunity lost. I will wrap my body in the polyester they require me to wear but do not provide, shackle the stones to my feet and kneel down bedside, brush the hair from her face and kiss her forehead before I push out into the gallows that leaves a piece of me every day hanging up there in the sun, rotting, as the vultures circle, and that piece I give never covers, never compensates, what I put in.

Have you ever seen them tear the speedway down? All those guys who gave their lives on it, all those guys who gave their lives off of it—just chasing it—and then the man comes in and makes it rubble and dust, subdivides it and sells it as a dream, makes one wonder if it's worth it, makes a man wonder if anything is worth it. They tell me I want this, and this is the path to having it. I just can't get over the idea that if this is our one ride on this sphere, I simply want it all.

I walk to the station in the streetlight-aided morning, invest my first hour's wages into the machine that grants me passage to and from the hamster's wheel, brush past the turnstile as it assigns me a number for the authority to count, and find a seat on a bench, staring at the white tiles on the far side of the tracks, and it smells like electricity and grease and hot metal and piss, yet I think of lilacs.

I think of lilacs and having it all.

Nashville

Nashville would do the trick.
Would shake the funk she was in
from the hell he put—
puts—
her through.
So she went.

No jewels on her fingers,
just that dollar store diamond
ring tucked in her clutch
Saturday night at the Opry.
   Jim Lauderdale
     Crystal Gayle
       Whispering Bill
Stars on the Ryman Circle
   Stars glistening in her eyes.
Those padded pews sparked a rebirth,
born again more authentically
than she could have even been
at any old tent revival.

Now that ring—
she brought it to Nashville
in the hopes that she could pawn it
for a couple dollars more
than what was offered back in her podunk.
She needed that couple dollars more.
She owed for the special
she had acquired

DARRIN JAMES

for protection
from the derelict who presented the ring.
Yet as the Opry bid goodnight to the world,
a new thought,
a childlike wonder,
a liberated dream.
Realizing she had a voice,
she just needed six strings

Now that ring—
on the books
was worth about as much as a derelict's words
and she knew this
yet she hoped
and prayed
      as if hers would stand out
      from all the other prayers
      emanating
      outta Nashville
      on a Saturday night
that a benevolent pawnbroker
who lusts for dollar store diamonds
would have a dusty, old Japanese guitar
that he couldn't stand to look at anymore.
And if a kiss sealed the deal
that'd make a helluva debut single
and she'd invite him to the Opry
so she could sing it to his face.

This she considered,
among the Saturday night Broadway crowds,
past every auto-tuned, skinny-jeaned,

neon-drenched, cowboy bar.
If they could—she reasoned—she could.
The Saturday night stars assured
she would.

On the Sunday morning sidewalks
along the sleeping streets of that city,
she found all the pawn shops closed.
Seemed as if there wasn't one open in all of Tennessee.
When she pulled on the locked handles,
she could see those guitars
behind the glass and the bars
just hanging up there,
dreams ripe for the taking,
religiously regulated out of reach.

With those blown-out taillights looking back,
she turns that two-hundred-thousand-mile Kia east to podunk.
Puts sixty more miles on the odometer
to get to that sterile white office Monday morning
and by lunch time, by the time the asks of "How was it?" subside,
the Opry winds that filled optimistic sails wane
as sixty more miles show up on the odometer.
That dreamy Opry serenade is silent,
not even a whisper of what could have been
remains.

The journals cite heart disease, cancer, and the flu
when addressing ways to die.
Never do they acknowledge *grim reality*
as the leading cause of death in America today.

Camaro

Mission trip.
That's what they called it.
A mission to do God's will,
God's work,
to rehabilitate the homes of the less fortunate.
A noble enough cause.

Truth be told
I really didn't care much about nobility or charity.
I really just wanted to see someplace else.
I wanted to see America.
So I sold candy bars to raise the funds necessary
to give up the week of summer before I turned sixteen
deep in Appalachia,
the place New York sends cameras
when imaging the plight of the American people,
when imaging the blight of America herself.

The hollers of Eastern Kentucky are truly gorgeous.
That the memory of those mid-summer days
as the church van wound its way
to the abode where God's will sent us
to put a roof on a single-wide,
cordially welcomed by a seemingly abled-bodied man
who then spent the day watching us labor
ten feet above the picnic table he sat at,
drinking blue and white cans and
telling those who would ask
about his car—

muscle car.
That late-seventies,
fire-starter red Camaro
that sat in the side yard.
I asked.
I was a week away from a driving permit.

Shortly before we broke for the day,
Ol' Wildcat finally found motivation
in the bottom of one of those cans.
He took his Camaro,
      racing up and down the road,
          spinning the thing around,
             "cutting doughnuts"
           —as boys my age call it—
until it quit
evidently broke
as he was so deep under the hood
that he didn't even acknowledge us as we left,
couldn't muster a wave
after we worked the day
to rehab his dwelling
on our own dime.

In returning the next morning,
the Camaro remained,
pushed slightly in the weeds.
And I eyed it longingly
as a boy would a muscle car
days before he turned driving age.
But there was work to be done,
a roof to be finished.

DARRIN JAMES

Well after we ascended the ladders
and renewed our labor,
that Wildcat emerged from below,
excitedly yelling up from his picnic table
and his blue and white can breakfast
about his last night,
rattling off the car parts he went and bought
to fix the Camaro he broke.

Disenchanted
is what I became
Although boys my age don't know
what to call that feeling.

The week before a boy turns sixteen,
he has an understanding of cost
and when the able-bodied man
on a Tuesday morning
is enjoying a canned breakfast,
bragging about his new chrome carburetor,
          intake manifold,
                    headers,
I wondered what I was doing there,
why I sold candy bars to be there.
Then again, I didn't come to rehabilitate;
I only came to see America.

Monster Truck

Recession.
Yeah, but what does that mean?
They never taught us that.
Then again, what did they teach
at the liberal arts college?
They sold us a bill of goods,
sold us a notion,
sold us a piece of paper
that we were led to believe would be the ticket,
the ticket to the universe,
to the dreams I dreamed.
So I bought that line
with Dad's money saved from the mill
and all of mine,
all that a child could save and earn
from spending a youth working three jobs at a clip.
When determined that I had given enough,
they gave me that ticket to the universe
and I ended up at a locked gate
with no one to take it
without knowing what a recession was.

But the mill was hiring.
Not the mill proper,
the temp agency for the mill,
same work,
no benefits.

DARRIN JAMES

On a late winter Tuesday night
I found myself in the parking lot—
      the same that Dad had
      driven to five days a week
      for thirty-seven years to that point,
      and would continue driving to for another ten—
staring at the steam stacks looming
in a quickly darkening sky
as the shift change came through the gap in the fence.

Night comes on so quickly
up in those mountains.

Mark that as the low point in a life.
In that moment I have never been more defeated,
not because I felt entitled,
not because I was some college boy
and I shouldn't have to do this,
not because I was above this,
not because I was better than this,
but because these were the gates
my father walked through every day,
bled his blood behind some days,
scarred his skin behind
left his hearing back there.
He did all of this
so I wouldn't have to.
Yet here I was
going through those same gates,
not even as a full-fledged employee,
just a temp-backer.

And of course they'd hire me,
pending a clear piss test,
having to report within 48 hours
to a clinic on a hill going out of town.

I sat in a corner drinking paper cups of water
across from a woman the size of two,
cartoon character shirt stretched over her.
She was there for the same thing and wasn't in a rush.
This I knew as she loudly said as much
in the direction of
a distant-eyed mountain man in the far corner.
        Thousand mile stare.
        Not even here.
But she kept talking,
telling a story about how she drove three hours
this one time
in a rainstorm
to a monster truck show
    – tickets won in a gas station drawing –
only to find out upon arrival
the show was the next day.
So they –
        she and two she birthed and one of their dads
            – slept in the car
And the rain never let up
the entirety of those two days.
But she got to see Grave Digger
she cackled in excitement.

The man continued staring
and I went to the window
with the hole cut in it
and said I was ready
if I could please have a cup.

Years later I met a man from Wessex
in the middle of a night of Staré Město drinking.
He broke from the typical line of drinking conversation
by asking the first American he had ever met
if the land of the free was all "picket fences"
like the television led him to believe.
I laughed.
        "Absolutely not."
He nodded
in an solemn "I knew I was lied to" sort of way.
Aren't we all in some way?

Cast Lots

I knew the answer
Knew it and didn't want to ask
The question I ended up asking
But I did
I asked
I asked hoping for another answer
One that was more palatable
Than the unpalatable
Answer that I knew
But I asked
I asked, "How did he…"
The patriarch of the family
Of the girl I was to marry
"…acquire the…
'Jap'
…uniform"
With the family photos
And personal effects in the pocket
That I was anecdotally told of
Just before Christmas dinner
The year I was introduced

A forgotten spoil
The uniform
I assumed
Was stashed away
In his widow's attic
In a quaint house
On a quiet street
Maintained lawns

DARRIN JAMES

Manicured flowers
Santa Ana winds
SoCal sun
Here, South Pacific is
A movie
A musical
At best, grandpa's forgotten memory

I did not inquire of its location
Instead asked the question
The question to which I knew the answer
But I asked anyway
When a quiet moment found us
And she looked at me
As if she never had thought about it
As if she always thought of war as clean
That enemy uniforms are acquired
In a humane sort of sterile way
That the spoils of war are
Like traded jerseys
At the end of a friendly game
Handed over with a handshake
Before the victory parade
To quaint houses
On quiet streets
She didn't have to answer
She could have just shrugged
But she answered
So nonchalant
So casual
"I guess he took it off him"
That's the answer I knew

In saying that
I wanted to know
If she knew
That the sons of Tokyo
Weren't known to surrender
Seppuku
But I recused myself
And smiled
And joked
When introduced to the family
       One day I might call mine.

Weeks later:
"There are people, organizations…"
I brought up
"…who work to give things like that back…"
Hoping for a glimmer of good
"…the *trophies* taken…"
Closure
"…to the families"
To come out of this

She said:
"I asked, we don't have it anymore…"
Repatriated?
"…he lost it in a poker game…"
Gravity
"…we think, we're not sure…"
No one wins
"…but we don't have it anymore"
My silence was not acceptance
I remained silent
In despair

DARRIN JAMES

They cast lots for his clothes
          As they have done for millennia
Cast lots for his garments
          As if we have really changed
They cast lots for his vesture
          This, what the preacher told us
          Every Easter Sunday morn
          We swearing could never be us
          Yet
These things therefore the soldiers did
          And the story grows old as it repeats
          The story grows old as it repeats

The Night We Met

The night we met, I walked her home,
blocks, if not miles
past my place, past the park,
into the suburbs, to be abruptly told
"goodnight."

In this sudden solitude, an anxious realization:
The tab was still open, AMEX still on file.
I walked back, alone,
blocks, if not miles
out of the 'burbs, past my place,
past the hookers, around the homeless,
over the chronics, dodging the drunks
to sign the slip, recover the card,
only to walk blocks back to my empty abode,
hours away from my morning shift.

Hindsight defines that night as emblematic
of our relationship
of the next three years.
A boy goes out of his way
to pick up the tab
to get the girl home safe
to be left abruptly
to pick up the pieces
to carry on as if nothing happened.

DARRIN JAMES

In happier times, she revealed
      when she first saw me, her initial thought was:
            "This one will do".
Alone in the abode tonight,
      reflecting on her line,
            I suppose I did.

Pennies

she never picked up heads-up pennies.
Those are supposed to be good luck.
she only took ones that rested tails up.
Explaining that her grandmother once told her
that someone less fortunate needed that luck
more than she did.
she took that to heart and never forgot the lesson.

With a smile,
I can see her toddler self being told that
out running errands with her grandma
in a sweltering strip-mall parking lot.
It may have been a comment made in passing,
something said to stop a child from picking up everything.
But it was a mindset that she harbored decades later.
On our sunset walks, she would only pocket those tails-up coins,
reasoning to my smirking self that the heads-up ones were lucky
and someone else needed the luck more than her.

It was heartbreakingly beautiful,
innocent,
pure.

DARRIN JAMES

This is where my mind went in the overnight hours
as I sat in the dark
outside the bathroom door
listening to her deal with the nausea
the doctor said would result from the medication;
helplessly angry at the cosmos
for bringing this fate on the girl
who never took a lucky penny for herself,
always leaving the fortune
for the less fortunate to find.

Later,
she asked why I remained so angry,
why I was bitter.
I addressed my contempt for it all,
for the situation which befell the girl
who was so kind
that she left lucky pennies for others.
she took a long quiet look at me
before looking away for a long quiet time.
she didn't look me in the eyes when she admitted:
"I've started picking up heads-up pennies."

Dogs and Angels

I've stopped praying to the heavens
having realized the angels don't listen
to mortal boys.

I've stopped praying to the angels
since that one stole my dog
three days before Christmas.

In this season,
       the season in which angels hark and sing,
the angel I knew best,
the angel I had faith in
subscribed to a scorched earth policy.
       Smeared soul.
             Shattered heart.
Stole my dog.

In awe of the powers,
the power of an angel,
through wet eyes
I pleaded
       as boys have been known to do
             when disaster befalls
                  and they haven't been praying,
      pleaded for her to leave my dog,
bargained
       as boys have been known to do
             in hopeless times
                  and they haven't prayed,
      bargained everything for her to spare my dog.

But boys' cries were not new to her.
she's heard the grievances,
she's heard the transgressions,
she's entertained the pleas
of a thousand desperate boys before.
And mine?
Mine were inconsequential.
Mine fell on deaf ears.
And with a look so calloused
from being prayed to
        preyed on,
she took my dog and flew away,
flew home
to the City of Angels
to her Mother Superior's beckoning
three days before Christmas.

Now, a mortal boy has no recourse
in opposition of a heavenly host,
especially in this the season of angels,
especially when Mother Superior beckons,
incentivizing her City of Angels repatriotization
with a guilt-and-gold-laden prize package.
I couldn't compete with that.
Not as a mortal boy.
she got everything she was told she wanted.
I just begged for my dog.
My buddy.
My best friend.
she stole him anyway,
never to hear again from that angel on high.

Left with the lesson that
angels aren't looking for forever,
she is only looking for a boy to ring the bell
so she can get her wings.

They've got names for girls like her.
They've got words for girls like that.
I just call her "angel,"
refusing to call out to them anymore,
wary of the power they yield.
Angels don't listen to mortal boys.

DARRIN JAMES

218B

Strange
how the passing of years brings a man
'round to the same place.

If not for the manifestation of aches
              in just realized body parts,
an old man would swear
he was still young,
that time hadn't passed.
As if that rental cabin
by the sea had been
        covered with an anti-aging serum,
        concocted of sea spray and charcoal smoke,
        bastioned then by thick coats of reapplied paint,
              had somehow foiled the space-time continuum,
                  had somehow fended off the passing of time.

Ah, but time had passed
as time always does.
There's not a defense formidable enough to stave it off.

A family now occupied that cabin
which for one quiet, rainy weekend was mine—
                                              ours.

With doors open,
party lights strung,
laughter in the air,
drinks in hand,
dinner on single-use plates,
that could have been mine,
                  could have been ours.

What do the savants say about ghosts?
Must they represent the deceased?
I submit this inquiry
as seeing that cabin anew,
I was overcome with a vision,
a vision of they who remained alive
yet no longer existed.

I saw that girl
and our dog
and the entirety of that quiet, rainy weekend,
listening to Rodriguez,
accompanied by the waves.
Time had passed
yet I was wholly engulfed in the way it was.
The way it could have been.
Visions of unrealized futures swarmed,
overwhelming a now old man.

In fear, I dropped my gaze,
turning to the cabin which I was now assigned
and I ran,
ran scared
as if I were once again a child
who had just seen a ghost.

Maybe in that moment I was.
Maybe in that moment I had.

DARRIN JAMES

That weekend
was the weekend before I offered on that four-bedroom,
envisioning a future filled with family,
hers or mine—
ours—
but the offer fell through
and we weren't so far behind.

She had her story.
                Wish I didn't know now,
She had her other story.
                 what I didn't know then.
And I had mine.
                          So it goes.
                          Like ghosts.

                       I aged a lifetime that summer alone.

Yet seeing that cabin anew
makes me question if time has even passed
or if any of it was even real:
Girls
and dogs.
Lost futures
and ghosts.
All ghosts
like smoke on the wind.
Try and capture it,
a fruitless grasp
and it's gone
as if it ever was.

Public Radio

Once upon a time,
after the dishes were washed,
the dog walked,
the clothes put out for the morning,
we'd lie in bed on Sunday evenings
in the dim lamp light
listening to Public Radio.

Those were the days I'd say,
"This is a pretty good life,"
and mean it.
Talking through the top of the hour news,
ignoring that real world,
wholly content in our own
in that bed
in the dim lamp light.

The Sunday routine
        for so long.
The Sunday routine
        until it wasn't.

DARRIN JAMES

For the first time in a long time
        for the first time since…
I cued the Public Radio this Sunday eve,
the lamp light,
the mattress,
the hum of the same nightstand fan,
all the same.
Yet, it seemed those shows,
once perfect bookends to the weekend,
had, like all good things, ceased.
"Pretty good" had gone.

It was always I,
getting up from the comfort of that queen,
to put the final period on the weekend,
reluctantly.
And she,
she would always pretend to sleep,
never kiss me goodnight,
leaving me wondering
how good those times were.

Remedy

Never has a dream played so vividly through my night,
so intense that in waking from it,
I tossed, then upon falling again, reengaged the vision.
It seemed to carry on for the entirety
of that single period of darkness.

> She had come back into my life
> with an infant child,
> a son
> she said was mine.
> And I?
> Cautiously elated.
> Happy.
> Happy to readjust course,
> accept, embrace this new purpose
> with her
> and a son of my own.

Then Helios brought about the day
and I haven't seen them since,
waking instead to a woman who
once told me she had a nightmare
in which she was carrying my child
and didn't know how to "remedy the situation."

Situation.

Remedy.

She wondered aloud
why I seemed so quiet,
so distant
that day.
I lied,
saying I felt ill.

If telling the truth,
I would have had to recall the dream,
which she would have called
a nightmare.
A situation,
needing a remedy.

Danny

A grandfather's final ask.
A best friend's dying wish.
My hero's last request.
Looking up with his big, blue eyes
into my same blue eyes,
he asks,
wishes,
requests,
"When you have a son… name him Danny."
His father's name.
And while his name has been passed,
there hadn't been another Danny.

It is believed that a great memory is desirable
but a great memory makes things hard to forget.

Thus a humble ask,
wish,
request,
from that old man
has proved impossible to forget,
a moral gnat
following me through time.
And as the decades pass,
a snag in my soul
as I haven't come through
since there hasn't been another Danny.

DARRIN JAMES

Out There

The road while long
has a way
of coming back around
to quiet streets in familiar villages.

Speaking loudly for his benefit,
I recounted the miles for that old man
in his quiet office,
walls lined with transportation artifacts
showing how the country moved
over the course of the last century.
Surely he would,
out of anyone in this quiet town,
appreciate stories of Rushmore,
of Old Faithful, Golden Gate, Rainier,
Grauman's Chinese,
Diamond Head west to the Rising Sun.
Assuming he had,
I asked if he had ever been.
Said the old man,
with a shake of his head:
"I never made it out there."
Nonchalant,
as if he missed the carnival
        but might make it next year.
As if he didn't watch the season finale
        but he'd catch it on rerun.
As if he were not at the right book end of life
        and this all could be reracked and played again.

Panic found me in that moment,
in the subtle harsh reality of his words.
We'll never see it all
and then it's over.
Back to ashes.
Back to stardust.

Eight months later,
after fighting through another bitter mountain winter,
the old man breathed his last breath
in a quiet room
on a quiet street
in a familiar village
on what will be remembered
as the prettiest day of spring.
I'll have to take their word for it though
as I
I remained adrift in unfamiliar waters,
calling unfamiliar ports,
seeking while seeking still permitted,
chasing so long as time graces
out there on life's road.

Little Red Dog

She said,
"I'm keeping the dog alive
until you get home."

I wanted to say,
"If the dog is ready,
let her go,"
not wanting her to suffer.

But I didn't.
I can't remember what I said
if anything.
What could be said?

She added:
"She's not ready.
She's waiting for you to get home."

Home.

When I left, she was young.
Then again, so was I.
How had the road gone on
for so long?
How had I been gone
for so long
that the little, red dog was
having to be kept alive?

Distance has no bearing on the passing of time.

As promised,
that little red dog was waiting
when the world spit me out
onto that mountain where I grew up,
where she grew old.
We sat on the porch
I held her bone,
wrapped her in a blanket,
set her on the couch,
let that old girl do
whatever she damn well pleased.

Then came the time
which forced my leave again
as that's what the world expects.
So I kissed her on the head,
thanked her for her love,
and told her it was okay
if this was goodbye.

I wasn't quite back
to where I was told to be
when the phone lit.
I knew right away.

In answering, she confirmed:
"She was waiting for you;
she held on to see you,"
as if I deserved that,
    as if I deserved the love
    of that little, red dog.

DARRIN JAMES

Battlefield Youth

The rage that was has waned,
the fire that burned, snuffed,
the battlefield, quiet
as I come to,
come up for air.

From the pockmarked field
that surrounds
a faint cawing, crying
rises
from unseen,
desperate men,
passed over, passing on.

O'er past the tree line,
the faint roar of the victors
already on their way home
to their beautiful wives,
home fires burning.

I check myself –
self-inspect.
The heart seems bruised,
        broken,
yet still beating.
The ears ring,
eyes clouded with scars,
yet
on a whole,

unscathed,
unencumbered,
unattached.

Amid the dying day,
I consider:
what is said about
the unwed, childless man
in his hometown
at the news of his passing?
Does anything get said?
Is he even remembered?

There's talk of work on the border,
work that no good man wants,
work that no holy man believes in,
but work that'll take a weary man
to that princesa's bed.

As the stars illuminate,
looking for direction,
I question:
pursue the battle
or a run to the border,
to her arms,
call myself a victor
with home fires of my own
as the vector?

DARRIN JAMES

In my dreams,
I oft find myself
walking
from the old town
up those hills
to the home where I grew up.

But I never get there
before I wake.

Rockingham

WNCW
  up the Blue Ridge
fading in and out
  on the Parkway.
Asheville by noon, if luck holds out.

WNCW
  fading in and out.
My only companion
  save for my thoughts.

I think of my grandfathers.
Wonder if they traveled these roads—
this road—
took in these views
with only the radio and their thoughts
to keep them company,

    Ten days and twenty-five hundred miles earlier:
      beers over a box of photos,
    assorted scraps of lives long since lived.
      I found out who they were,
        who I am.

    Driving desires made more sense.
      Postcards and roadmaps.
    Oklahoma, before the Dust Bowl.
      Depression Era Florida.
        The Badlands.

DARRIN JAMES

A story about selling the headlights
for gas money to get home.
Back on those roads,
back in that time.

After the road-trip revelations,
a marriage realization.
One wed at twenty-nine.
The other?
Thirty-three.
Back in those days,
back in that time.

Which made me feel predestined,
comforted,
in my current disposition
with only notebooks and the camera in the passenger seat.

Whomever is scripting this life of mine
will never be able to ascribe
"Traditional Love Story"
as the title to mine
if a love story is what I even get.

To have a partner is to share a life.
To share memories with
— a life witness.
Yet stories and pictures will be all I can share
with that "I don't want to go" girl
under the auspices
that we'll get there—back here—someday
when we have the time

as if we'll ever have enough time,
as if a lifetime is ever enough time
to see color find its way to the leaves of the Blue Ridge,
to wear the hats, hanging in Asheville bar-b-que joints,
to feel heartbreak as WNCW fades for the final
as Virginia comes into view.

Come nightfall, I'll beddown
between the interstate and the Baptist college.
In that moment,
alone in that room,
the "I don't want to go" girl calls
saying she was done with my rambling.
Was there something I had to say?

Just…

No…

Only
a sigh,
a "good-luck,"
another "good-bye."

What did she expect?
I'm a jaded old spirit,
calloused old heart,
soul covered in a life's patina.

The act of hawking the headlights
to stay on the road
is in my blood.

DARRIN JAMES

I've watched my heroes die,
taken those calls,
buried the bodies.
I've lost what I understood to be love.
Still question what that word means.
Her leaving?
It'll shake.
It'll hurt.
But come morning light,
put a fresh coat over the patina
and go on to Rockingham.

Walnut

In a wandering
lifetime
none had felt
so much like home
as that place

Open window breezes,
the jets thrust
at Lindberg,
locomotives thunder,
rolling toward
old Mexico

Saturday nights
the old console radio
quietly entertaining
as we sat on the hardwood,
listening

In a wandering
lifetime
I felt no greater peace
as in that place

All the sounds once loud
out in the distance
now quiet
within those walls

Yet, when voices got loud
it was as if there was no sound

DARRIN JAMES

No one was listening

No one could comprehend

No one heard a thing

When she set me aside
she chided that I
wouldn't think
about her anymore

I harbored an opposing sentiment
choosing not to offer
as no one was listening

That sentiment,
these years later,
now validated
I'll offer:

Alice –
Some nights
In my dreams
I walk those streets
Through the gate
Up the stairs
To find you
Leaned against the sofa
Quietly listening to that console.

Your smile
In that moment
Feels like home

Boxes

Black sheep.
Singular.
Solo.
One and only.
Yours truly.

Rebel.
They call me "rebel,"
seemingly so far from their convention
that I have warranted this moniker
in their minds.

That line they walk—
       are told to walk—
              and do so happily
                   without question
is
so
nar-
row,
is
so
fine,

engrained
so deep in the psyche.
Deviations are unfathomable.

DARRIN JAMES

They fear the berms,
love the white lines
that tell them what to do
while I use the median to pass,
pass convention.
Convention shrieks at my newly forged path.
Convention reviles any deviation,
reports any misstep,
questions my every question.
And I question.
I questioned the teachers in that sand, brick school.
I questioned the preachers in that stacked stone church.
I question—challenge—society in all their glass houses.
I could never understand these boxes,
their boxes,
all boxes,
all their neat square corners
and boxes.

Now if I may be so bold,
as bold is how they see me,
I tender an addendum
to the only guarantees in life:
death and taxes.
Add:
boxes.

Shipping boxes.
                              Mail boxes.
          Lock boxes.
                              Cable Boxes.
              Don't think outside of the boxes.
              Have opinions on batters' boxes.
                         Jewelry boxes for a happy wife.
                         Confession boxes for eternal life.

Drive your boxes
      to your boxes
            to pay the night deposit boxes
                  to occupy your boxes,
                      aspiring for bigger boxes
                          to keep up with your neighbors' boxes.
And after all these boxes
they'll take what remains
and box it up,
hide it six feet in the earth.
Boxes.
Boxes for eternity
'til kingdom come.

When the psychopomps do find me,
if it is Charon,
I believe a coin will not be sought.
If it is Pete,
I believe his scroll will be set aside.
Instead of a token demanded,
I expect to be asked one question.

DARRIN JAMES

Not, "What did you worship?"
Not, "What did you believe?"
Not, "What basket did your alms line?"
Not, "Where did you reside?"
I will be asked,
"Where is your proof of life?"
The answer to which
will not come from a box.
The answer to which I expect
will come from a life lived
avoiding boxes.

Green Flash

The point –
I struggle with that.
On a grand enough scale,
        a realistic one in the course of time
I question to see.

All the truths we hold dear
        will be disproven.
The mountains we struggle to ascend
        will be blown back to the cosmos.
The work we center our lives around
        will be for not.
The borders we defend with blood
        will be erased, redefined.
The languages we speak
        will be muted.
The knowledge of the universe
        will be ignored.
The idols we worship—kill for—
        will become false, forgotten.
On a long enough timeline,
I struggle to see the purpose.
Man is just a flash—the first light of a spark—
on the long dark line of time.
Man is merely the green flash
over the course of a day.

DARRIN JAMES

So few watch the setting sun,
appreciate it,
stuck in their tract houses
with heavily mortgaged views
of their neighbor's kitchen walls.
Once told to want it all,
they end up in sterile asylums,
dreaming someone else's dream
of what could have been.

They
cannot be bothered
to look at the stars
as the radiant glow
of their television sets
light the landscape.
They
can tell you about serial episodes,
have opinions of advertisements,
invest in fantasy sport teams,
collect collectible figurines.
They
live in the land of debt
claim perfect vision
in the fog of make-believe.
They
cannot navigate without a tow,
cannot find true north.
They
have never seen the Dipper,
can't see past the powerlines
looming over the front yard.

I wonder what we've missed.
I question if any of us are
who we actually think we are.
They
aren't thinking though.
They
act as if they've just been injected in time.
They
act as if they'll carry on forever.

Like a siren,
she coos and consoles,
tries to quiet my mind,
claiming aloud that I think too much.
Just come to bed.
"Here... watch this,"
wanting me to stare at her
instead of watching the green flash,
chasing the green flash,
pulling me away from the skies,
the stars,
life.

www.ingramcontent.com/pod-product-compliance
Lightning Source LLC
Chambersburg PA
CBHW070536030426
42337CB00016B/2231